DISCOVERING DINOSAURS
SMALL & SCARY

INTERNET LINKED

MICHAEL BENTON
Chrysalis Education

INTERNET SAFETY

Always follow these guidelines for a fun and safe
journey through cyberspace:

1. Ask your parents for permission before you go online.

2. Spend time with your parents online
and show them your favorite sites.

3. Mail your family's e-mail address, even if you have your own
(only give your personal address to someone you trust).

4. Do not reply to e-mails if you feel
they are strange or upsetting.

5. Do not use your real last name when you are online.

6. Never try to meet "cyber friends" in person
without your parents' permission.

7. Never give anyone your password.

8. Never give anyone your home address and telephone number.

9. Do not send scanned pictures of yourself
unless your parents approve.

10. Leave a website right away if you find something that is
offensive or upsetting. Talk to your parents about it.

Every effort has been made to ensure none of the recommended websites in this book is linked to inappropriate material. However, due to the ever-changing nature of the Internet, the publishers regret they cannot take responsibility for future content of these websites. Therefore, it is strongly advised that children and parents consider the safety guidelines above.

U.S. publication copyright © 2003 Chrysalis Education.
International copyright reserved in all countries.

Distributed in the United States by
Smart Apple Media, 1980 Lookout Drive, North Mankato, MN 56003

Copyright © 2002 Chrysalis Books PLC

Author: Prof. Michael Benton
Consultant: Dougal Dixon BSc (Hons), MSc
Illustrator: John Sibbick
Digital Retouch Artist: Steve Sweet

Editorial Director: Honor Head
Art Director: Simon Rosenheim
Senior Editor: Rasha Elsaeed
Project Editor: Jane Yorke
Assistant Editor: Clare Chambers
Project Designer: Sarah Crouch
Assistant Designers: Keren-Orr Greenfeld, Zeta Jones

ISBN 1-93233-359-2
Library of Congress Control Number 2003102611

Printed and bound in Taiwan

CONTENTS

FEARSOME MINIBEASTS

Not all dinosaurs were huge. Some of the smallest, fastest, and fiercest dinosaurs were smaller than you are.

The first dinosaurs were tiny. The smallest baby dinosaur was *Mussaurus,* a tiny prosauropod from the Late Triassic Period. *Mussaurus* was about the size of a kitten, and were only eight inches long. The smallest adult dinosaur was the meat-eating *Compsognathus* from the Late Jurassic Period. It measured about 28 inches long—about the same as a medium-sized dog, although it weighed much less.

Small reptiles often lived alongside the biggest dinosaurs ever to have roamed earth, such as the 72-foot-long *Brachiosaurus.* Small dinosaurs like *Compsognathus* survived because they were skillful predators. Others were successful because they had well-developed defense systems and could outrun, and possibly outwit, the larger beasts of their day.

Theropods

Some of the scariest dinosaurs were small meat-eating theropods. Vulturelike ornithomimids were light, fast-moving hunters. Their strong hands had either fingers or claws. They used their hands to grasp and hold down their wriggling prey.

Struthiomimus

Oviraptor

FACTFILE: THE DINOSAUR AGE

- The Mesozoic Era lasted from 250 to 65 million years ago. Mesozoic means "middle life."

- The Cretaceous Period lasted from 150 to 65 million years ago. Cretaceous comes from the Latin *creta* ("chalk").

- The Jurassic Period lasted from 205 to 150 million years ago. It was named after the Jura Mountains, France.

- The Triassic Period lasted from 250 to 205 million years ago. Triassic means "three-part."

Anchisaurus

Prosauropods

Dog-sized Anchisaurus was one of the first vegetarian dinosaurs. It had a long, strong and whiplike tail to defend itself.

Tenontosaurus

Dryosaurus

Ornithopods

Like many plant-eating ornithopods, birdlike hypsilophodontids had powerful legs and strong, balancing tails to help them run swiftly.

Hypsilophodon

Dromiceiomimus

Ceratopsians

As a bipedal dinosaur with a parrot-shaped beak and strong, grasping hands, Psittacosaurus could feed from trees, as well as low-lying plants. Unlike the horn-faced, tank-shaped Triceratops, early ceratopsians were human-sized and horn-free.

Psittacosaurus

LIVING DINOSAURS?

Some small dinosaurs have skeletons almost identical to *Archaeopteryx*—the oldest known bird. *Archaeopteryx* was one of the most famous fossil finds. It showed that dinosaur ancestors of birds must have developed the ability to fly. *Archaeopteryx* fossils date from the Late Jurassic Period and were found in Germany. The fossils clearly show the skeleton and delicate outlines of the feathers, which were preserved as soft imprints in the ancient mud.

When the first *Archaeopteryx* fossil was found in 1861, it provided the "missing link" in the story of evolution between reptiles and birds. Paleontologists had always thought that birds evolved from reptiles. They pointed to clues, such as the scales on a bird's legs. But the *Archaeopteryx* discovery provided much stronger evidence. *Archaeopteryx* was a bird with feathers and wings, but it also had some dinosaur features, such as teeth, claws, and a long, bony tail. In fact, the skeleton of *Archaeopteryx* is remarkably similar to the little theropod—*Compsognathus*.

Archaeopteryx *fossil*
The first bird had wings that were identical in structure to the wings of a modern bird. The first bird had long, fingerlike feathers. The wing muscles would not have been as strong as a modern bird, but the flying action was probably the same

Dinosaurs and birds
The skeletons below show how Archaeopteryx compares to a modern pigeon. The main difference is that modern birds do not have teeth or tails. Therefore birds' bodies are lighter and more suitable for flying.

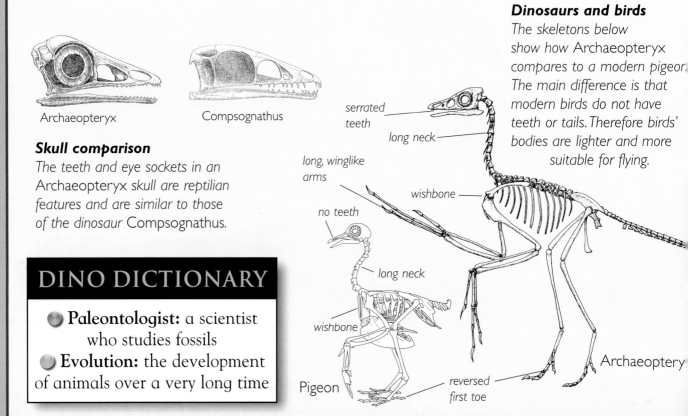

Archaeopteryx   Compsognathus

Skull comparison
The teeth and eye sockets in an Archaeopteryx skull are reptilian features and are similar to those of the dinosaur Compsognathus.

serrated teeth
long neck
long, winglike arms
no teeth
long neck
wishbone
wishbone
Pigeon
reversed first toe
Archaeopteryx

DINO DICTIONARY

● **Paleontologist:** a scientist who studies fossils
● **Evolution:** the development of animals over a very long time

Early bird

In life, Archaeopteryx would have looked like a bird. But it had not evolved with many of the weight-saving devices of modern birds, such as the beak and the stumpy tail.

INTERNET LINKS

http://www.chirpingbird.com/netpets/html/classrm/archeopx.html
A short, fun account of *Archaeopteryx*, with some good links.

http://www.talkorigins.org/faqs/archaeopteryx/info.html
This site has pictures of all the *Archaeopteryx* specimens, plus details of their discovery and what they mean.

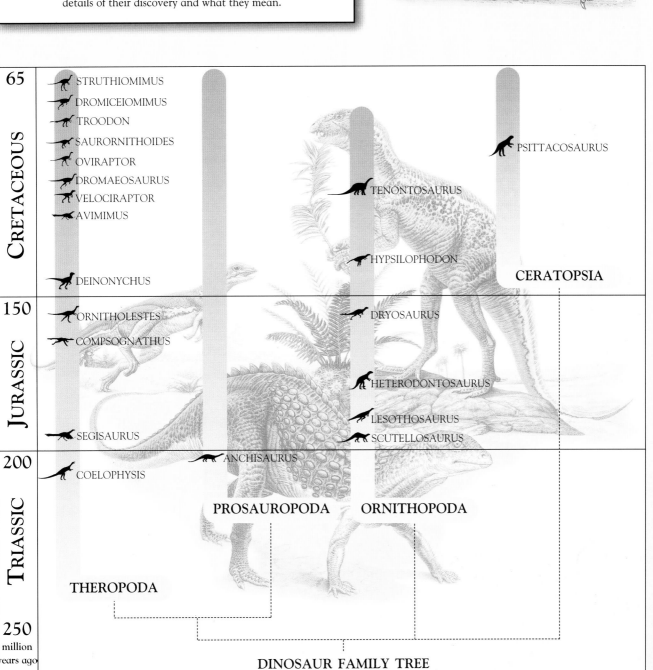

65	STRUTHIOMIMUS	
	DROMICEIOMIMUS	
CRETACEOUS	TROODON	
	SAURORNITHOIDES	PSITTACOSAURUS
	OVIRAPTOR	
	DROMAEOSAURUS	TENONTOSAURUS
	VELOCIRAPTOR	
	AVIMIMUS	
		HYPSILOPHODON
	DEINONYCHUS	CERATOPSIA
150	ORNITHOLESTES	DRYOSAURUS
JURASSIC	COMPSOGNATHUS	
		HETERODONTOSAURUS
		LESOTHOSAURUS
	SEGISAURUS	SCUTELLOSAURUS
200	ANCHISAURUS	
	COELOPHYSIS	
TRIASSIC	PROSAUROPODA	ORNITHOPODA
	THEROPODA	
250 million years ago		

DINOSAUR FAMILY TREE

PATTERNS & FEATHERS

Small dinosaurs may have been just as successful at hunting prey as large dinosaurs.

It is difficult to know how dinosaurs looked, because fossils cannot tell us about the color of their skin. Many reptiles today, such as lizards and snakes, have colorful skin patterns. Some dinosaurs might have been the same. Colorful skin patterns would have helped to ward off bigger predators. *Segisaurus*—a small theropod and a relative of *Coelophysis*—is shown here with colorful body stripes. Another intriguing theropod was *Avimimus*. Its skeleton interested scientists because of its mixture of birdlike and dinosaur features. The fossil of *Avimimus* showed that the dinosaur had a ridge along the arm bones. Birds have a similar structure to fix their feathers in place. As a result, scientists believe that many dinosaurs were feathered.

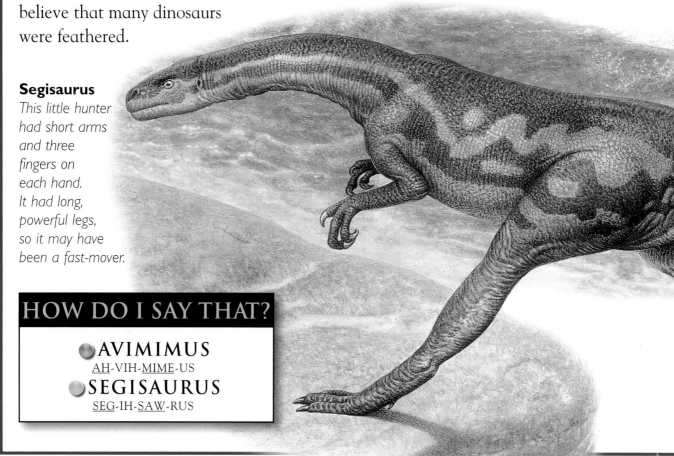

Segisaurus
This little hunter had short arms and three fingers on each hand. It had long, powerful legs, so it may have been a fast-mover.

HOW DO I SAY THAT?

⬤**AVIMIMUS**
AH-VIH-MIME-US

⬤**SEGISAURUS**
SEG-IH-SAW-RUS

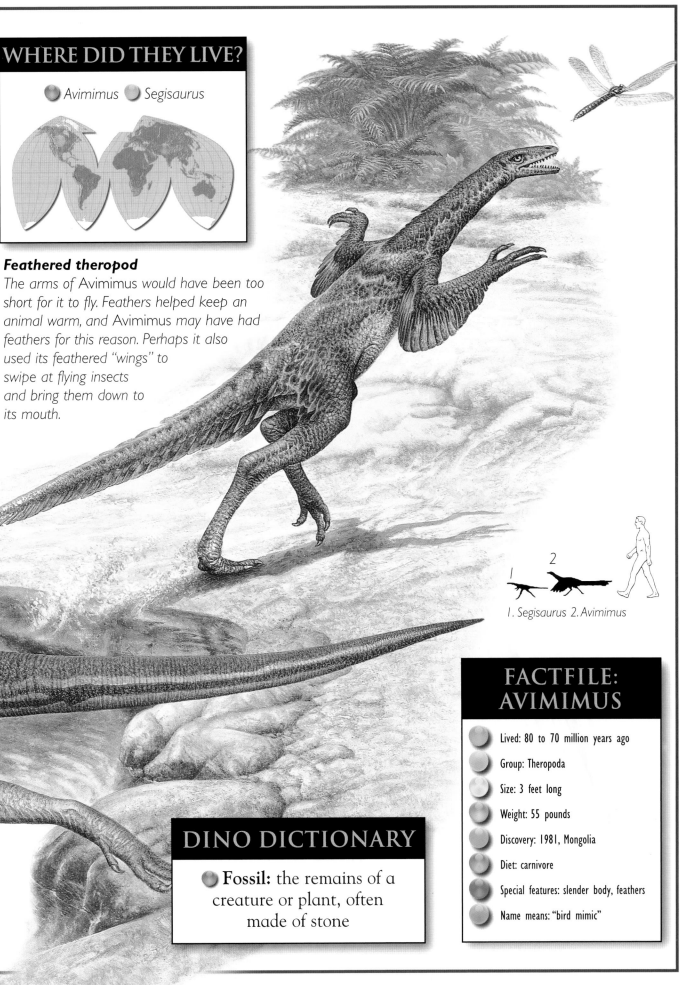

Feathered theropod

The arms of Avimimus would have been too short for it to fly. Feathers helped keep an animal warm, and Avimimus may have had feathers for this reason. Perhaps it also used its feathered "wings" to swipe at flying insects and bring them down to its mouth.

1. Segisaurus 2. Avimimus

DINO DICTIONARY

⬤ **Fossil:** the remains of a creature or plant, often made of stone

FACTFILE: AVIMIMUS

⬤ Lived: 80 to 70 million years ago

⬤ Group: Theropoda

⬤ Size: 3 feet long

⬤ Weight: 55 pounds

⬤ Discovery: 1981, Mongolia

⬤ Diet: carnivore

⬤ Special features: slender body, feathers

⬤ Name means: "bird mimic"

FLESH-EATERS

Tryannosaurus rex **was a fearsome predator, but small predatory theropods were just as fierce.**

The first dinosaurs were small, fast-running, meat-eating theropods. Theropods ("beast feet") walked on two back legs and had sharp claws on their hands and birdlike feet. They used their hands to grab their prey, and possibly to carry pieces of meat to devour later.

Coelphysis was one of the earliest theropods. *Ornitholestes* and *Compsognathus* came later in the Late Jurassic. All three reptiles had similar features and habits. They had slender bodies, long flexible necks, powerful legs, sharp teeth, and strong clawed hands. Groups of *Coelphysis* fossils were found in North America. This suggests that these agile dinosaurs may have hunted in packs, like wild wolves today. Since the fossils were found in a group, these dinosaurs may have died together in a drought.

1. *Compsognathus* 2. *Ornitholestes*
3. *Coelophysis*

HOW DO I SAY THAT?

● COELOPHYSIS
SEEL-OH-FY-SIS

● COMPSOGNATHUS
KOMP-SOG-NAY-THUS

● ORNITHOLESTES
OR-NITH-OH-LESS-TEEZ

Sharp-toothed hunter
Ornitholestes had sharp teeth that pointed inward, trapping prey in its mouth. This dinosaur may have snatched flesh from prey that had been killed by larger dinosaurs.

Slim and ferocious

Coelophysis *was a small but merciless predator. A skeleton of a younger dinosaur was found in the stomach of an adult.*

Small and speedy

Compsognathus *was one of the smallest dinosaurs. It was about as big as a cat.* Compsognathus *was an active predator; it chased small prey, such as lizards and insects. Its two-fingered hands were unusual for dinosaurs of the time.*

WHERE DID THEY LIVE?

- Coelophysis and Ornitholestes
- Compsognathus

THE OSTRICH DINOSAURS

Ornithomimids were fast-running, meat-eating hunters but, strangely enough, they had no teeth.

Why didn't the ornithomimids have teeth? They may have eaten food, such as insects and eggs, for which teeth were not needed. It is also likely that the ornithomimids had sharp-edged beaks, like modern eagles and vultures. These beaks were used to kil prey by tearing up the flesh.

Struthiomimus
With its speedy legs and strong hands, Struthiomimus may have hunted insects, such as dragonflies. Struthiomimus was probably too big an animal to survive on just insects, however. It is likely it also hunted lizards and other small animals.

Coming to get you!
Ostrich dinosaurs had long, strong fingers with claws to grab small animals and tear them apart.

HOW DO I SAY THAT?

- **DROMICEIOMIMUS**
  DROM-IK-AY-OH-MIME-US
- **OVIRAPTOR**
  OVE-IH-RAP-TOR
- **STRUTHIOMIMUS**
  STROOTH-EE-OH-MIME-US

1. Oviraptor
2. Struthiomimus
3. Dromiceiomimus

Dromiceiomimus and Struthiomimus
Oviraptor

Strange head
Oviraptor *had an unusual skull with a hornlike structure over its snout. The purpose of this nose horn is not known.*

Dromiceiomimus
This dinosaur was a close relative of Struthiomimus *but it had a shorter back and more slender legs. When* Dromiceiomimus *chased its prey, it tucked up its arms and stuck its tail out stiffly to act as a counterbalance.*

Run like a horse
Ornithomimids appeared in the Late Cretaceous Period. They had long, slender back legs like modern ostriches. They may have run at speeds of 31 miles per hour— as fast as a race horse.

Egg thief?
Although Oviraptor *was not a true ornithomimid, it was feathered just like an bird.* Oviraptor *("egg thief") was named when the first fossils were found near nests in Mongolia. Recent studies have shown that these nests actually belonged to* Oviraptor. *The dinosaur was looking after its own eggs, not stealing them!*

FACTFILE: STRUTHIOMIMUS

Lived: 75 to 65 million years ago

Group: Theropoda

Size: 10 to 13 feet long

Weight: 220 pounds

Discovery: 1917, Alberta, Canada

Diet: carnivore

Special features: long powerful legs, toothless jaws

Name means: "ostrich mimic"

BIG-EYED RUNNERS

Dinosaurs had very small brains in relation to the size of their bodies. But the troodontids had some of the largest brains of all the dinosaurs.

Troodontids like *Saurornithoides* and *Troodon* were fast-moving, lightly built theropods. Their bodies were similar to the ornithomimids. They had ostrichlike necks, small heads, long legs, and tails. But troodontids had stronger hands and feet, with huge slashing claws.

For their body size, troodontids had brains that were bigger than the normal size for dinosaurs. This could mean they may have been the most intelligent! By filling a fossil skull with dry lentils, then pouring them into a measuring jug, scientists have figured out the size of many dinosaur's brains.

WHERE DID THEY LIVE?

● *Saurornithoides* ● *Troodon*

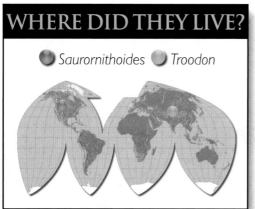

Knifelike claws
Saurornithoides used the claws on its feet to kill its prey. It grabbed small mammals and lizards, and held them tight while tearing the flesh with its teeth. This dinosaur had to rely on its hands and feet, because its teeth were very small and could not have been used to kill its prey.

14

1. Troodon   2. Saurornithoides

Big, beady eyes

Troodon *had big, beady eyes set high up on the snout, so it could look forward as well as sideways. Most dinosaurs had their eyes set on the side of their heads like a horse, so each eye saw a different scene. Troodontids may have been able to see in three dimensions like we can.*

HOW DO I SAY THAT?

SAURORNITHOIDES
SAWR-OR-NITH-OIDE-EEZ

TROODON
TROO-DON

THE SLASHERS

The dromaeosaurids may have been human-sized dinosaurs, but their sickle-shaped claw on the second toe of each foot made them ferocious monsters.

The first dromaeosaurid fossils were found about 100 years ago, but scientists could not tell what these dinosaurs looked like because the fossils were incomplete. Then, in 1964, full skeletons of *Deinonychus* were found in North America. *Deinonychus* had good eyesight and a large head, so it probably had a relatively big brain for a dinosaur. It had long legs and arms, and a stiff tail for balance, so it may have been a fast runner. *Velociraptor* can be distinguished from *Deinonychus* and *Dromaeosaurus* by its low, narrow head. The differences in head shape may reflect differences in the diets of these dinosaurs.

However, the most interesting feature of a dromaeosaurid was its huge, slashing claws. When it attacked prey, *Deinonychus* balanced on one foot, raised its other leg, and flicked the claw—tearing a huge gash down the side of its victim. This allowed small predators like *Deinonychus* to attack much larger plant-eating dinosaurs.

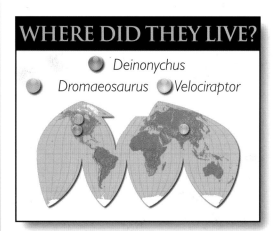

WHERE DID THEY LIVE?

- Deinonychus
- Dromaeosaurus
- Velociraptor

Dromaeosaurus

Little is known about Dromaesosaurus, the first dromaeosaurid. Only parts of the skull and a few leg bones were found in 1914. Scientists put the rest of the skeleton together when complete fossils of Deinonychus were found.

Big mouth

The jaws of Deinonychus were lined with many backward-pointing teeth. Prey could not escape once it was in the dinosaur's teeth. If it struggled, the animal just moved further down the dinosaur's throat.

FACTFILE: DEINONYCHUS

- Lived: 110 to 100 million years ago
- Group: Theropoda
- Size: 10 feet long, 5 feet tall
- Weight: 165 pounds
- Discovery: 1964, Montana
- Diet: carnivore
- Special features: slashing claw, stiff tail
- Name means: "terrible claw"

Caught in the act

Velociraptor *was an extremely efficient predator—better than many larger predators. A fossil from Mongolia shows a Velociraptor locked in a fight with a horned dinosaur called Protoceratops. Velociraptor is shown grasping the head shield of Protoceratops. This suggests that these dinosaurs probably died together in a freak sandstorm. The remains of Velociraptor were not found with Dromaeosaurus and Deinonychus. It is unlikely that they all lived together as shown in this picture.*

1. Dromaeosaurus
2. Velociraptor
3. Deinonychus

HOW DO I SAY THAT?

DEINONYCHUS
DINE-ON-IKE-US

DROMAEOSAURUS
DROM-AY-OH-SAW-RUS

VELOCIRAPTOR
VEL-OSS-IH-RAP-TOR

SMALL THEROPODS

Every part of the skeleton of a small theropod was designed for quick movement and effective hunting. The skull was narrow and the jaws were powerful. The neck was long and flexible to allow the dinosaur to thrust and dive its head like a snake. The hands were strong, so predators could wrestle their prey to the ground. The legs were long, agile, and powerful and designed for running. The whiplike tail provided balance when these predators pursued their fast-moving prey.

Light headed
Like Compsognathus, Coelophysis *had a hollow skull and long jaws lined with serrated teeth.*

The first theropods
Coelophysis *was one of the earliest theropods. It had many features that were similar to other small theropods. It had long arms and relatively short legs, so it could rest on all fours when it fed.*

Compsognathus

Coelophysis

Strong hands
Coelophysis *had fingers on each hand, so it could grasp its prey effectively.*

Nimble predator
Compsognathus *was one of the smallest dinosaurs that ever lived. It had a slender, pointed snout so it could dig deep inside the animal carcass to strip of the meat.*

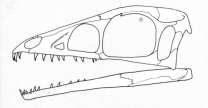

Compsognathus *skull*
This hollow skull was typical of a predator that caught small, fast-moving animals, such as lizards and insects.

Clawed hands
Long-fingered hands were better at grasping prey, so it is unusual for a small predator like Compsognathus to have short hands with claws.

Running legs
Compsognathus *had long, slender legs typical of small, fast-moving dinosaurs. This dinosaur had three long, forward-pointing toes on each foot, as well as a backward-pointing fourth toe.*

Fingers and thumbs

Ornitholestes *had long hands with powerful fingers. It may have used them to control its struggling prey. The dinosaur had two long fingers and a short first finger. It probably gripped its prey, using the short finger like a thumb.*

INTERNET LINKS

http://www.inhandmuseum.com
Click on "Dinosaurs" and enter the exhibit hall of the virtual museum of natural history.

http://www.ucmp.berkeley.edu/education/dinolink.html
Find out about the main groups of theropods.

http://www.enchantedlearning.com/subjects/dinosaurs
A giant kids' dictionary about dinosaurs and their times.

Big biter

Ornitholestes *had a heavier skull than some of its relatives. It had a short, compact snout and more robust teeth, so it is likely* Ornitholestes *had a stronger bite than* Compsognathus *and* Coelophysis.

Ornitholestes

Balancing act

The long tails of these dinosaurs stuck out straight behind them and provided a counterbalance as they ran.

Meat- or plant-eater?

Some small theropods, such as the ornithomimids like Struthiomimus, *had no teeth in their mouths. These dinosaurs may have fed on plants—grasping branches in their strong fingers and tearing off the leaves with their jaws. However, this would have been an unusual diet for a theropod—most were meat-eating predators. Scientists have not found clear evidence to prove whether they were meat- or plant-eaters. They may have lived on both animal flesh and vegetation.*

ANATOMY OF A KILLER

Deinonychus was a perfect hunter. Every part of its body—from the tip of its snout to the end of its tail—was designed for speed and ferocity. But the dinosaur's key weapon was the slashing claw on each foot. This required more skill than that shown by any other dinosaur. *Deinonychus* may been good at keeping balance and probably had excellent eyesight as well. It could stand on one leg, slash its victim with the other claw, land back on both feet, and twist around, ready to strike again.

Claw movement for attacking　　*Claw position for running*

Vicious weapon
Instead of using its teeth like a typical predator, Deinonychus' main weapons were its legs and its huge claws. When Deinonychus ran, it held its slashing foot upright. However, it could swing its foot through more than 180 degrees to attack its prey.

Deinonychus

Head
The high skull shows that Deinonychus had powerful jaw muscles.

THE THEROPODS:

- *Avimimus*
- *Coelophysis*
- *Compsognathus*
- *Deinonychus*
- *Dromaeosaurus*
- *Dromiceiomimus*
- *Ornitholestes*
- *Oviraptor*
- *Saurornithoides*
- *Segisaurus*
- *Troodon*
- *Struthiomimus*
- *Velociraptor*

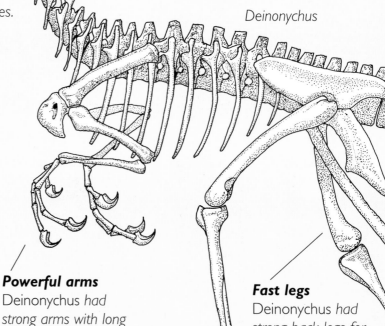

Powerful arms
Deinonychus had strong arms with long fingers for grasping its prey.

Fast legs
Deinonychus had strong back legs for running and a stiff tail that acted like a balancing rod.

Hunting

It is likely that Deinonychus hunted large prey in a pack and smaller prey on its own (left). A fossil skeleton of Tenontosaurus—a dinosaur ten times bigger than Deinonychus—was discovered surrounded by several Deinonychus. So five or six Deinonychus may have attacked a larger animal (as shown below)—like a pack of wild dogs do today.

1. Deinonychus runs up fast from behind as it hunts a smaller dinosaur.

2. Deinonychus leaps on the back of its prey, and sinks its teeth into the soft neck muscles.

Flexible and rigid

Deinonychus had a short, strong back. This allowed it to twist and turn effectively when it hunted. Its tail consisted of fine, bony rods that made it stiff.

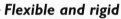

3 The killing claw rips the victim's belly open, and Deinonychus begins its feast.

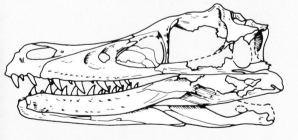

Similar relative

Velociraptor was a relative of Deinonychus, but it had a much flatter skull. Despite the differences in their skulls, the skeletons of the two dinosaurs are very similar, although Velociraptor was half the size of Deinonychus. This fossilized skull is slightly crushed—you can see how some of the bones do not fit exactly.

DINO DICTIONARY

- **Prey:** an animal that is hunted
- **Predator:** a flesh-eating hunter
- **Carcass:** the dead body of an animal
- **Skull:** the bones of the head

AMAZING ANCHISAURUS

Among the first small plant-eating dinosaurs to appear on earth were the prosauropods from the Late Triassic Period.

The first prosauropods were small reptiles, even though their later relatives—sauropods like *Apatosaurus* and *Diplodocus*—were giants. One of the smallest prosauropods was *Anchisaurus*. It was the height of a terrier dog but much longer. Fossils of *Anchisaurus* were actually the first dinosaur remains to be found in North America. *Anchisaurus* was lightly built and agile enough to escape quickly from the predatory dinosaurs of its day.

Head and hands
Anchisaurus had a small head and a long neck. Its teeth were small and pencil-shaped, so it probably fed on leaves from bushes and small trees. Anchisaurus *had five toes on each foot, and its broad thumb was armed with a large claw that was used to grasp plants.*

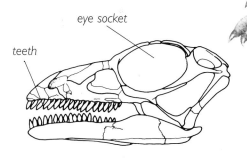

eye socket

teeth

Skull
Anchisaurus had a very large eye socket. Its teeth were coarsely serrated and packed tightly together for grinding up tough plants.

HOW DO I SAY THAT?

⬤ **ANCHISAURUS**
AN-KIH-SAW-RUS

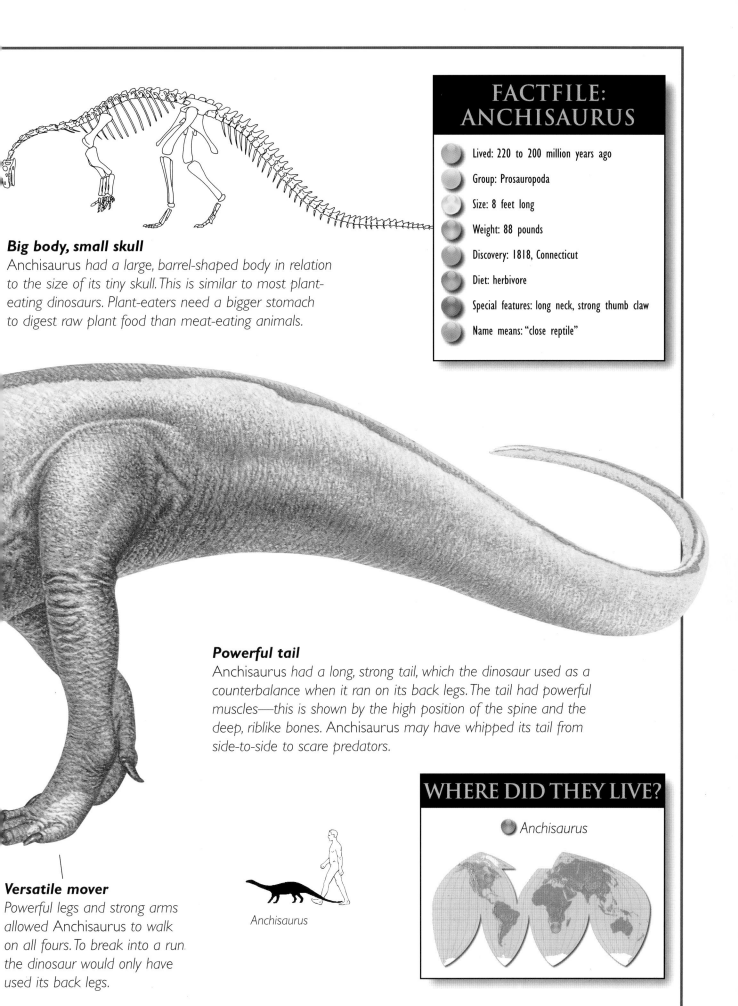

Big body, small skull
Anchisaurus *had a large, barrel-shaped body in relation to the size of its tiny skull. This is similar to most plant-eating dinosaurs. Plant-eaters need a bigger stomach to digest raw plant food than meat-eating animals.*

Powerful tail
Anchisaurus *had a long, strong tail, which the dinosaur used as a counterbalance when it ran on its back legs. The tail had powerful muscles—this is shown by the high position of the spine and the deep, riblike bones.* Anchisaurus *may have whipped its tail from side-to-side to scare predators.*

Versatile mover
Powerful legs and strong arms allowed Anchisaurus *to walk on all fours. To break into a run the dinosaur would only have used its back legs.*

Anchisaurus

WHERE DID THEY LIVE?

Anchisaurus

DINOSAUR DEFENSES

The main group of small, plant-eating dinosaurs were the ornithopods. Some had unusual armor and eating habits.

The first ornithopods lived during the Late Triassic Period. They were small, fast-moving, two-legged animals. The earliest ornithopod was *Lesothosaurus*, which was about the size of a cat. It could dart quickly to escape predators. Its head was primitive and lizardlike compared to later ornithopods. Its larger relative, *Scutellosaurus*, had rows of armor plates along its body. These were set into the skin like the bony scales of a crocodile.

   Heterodontosaurus was similar to *Lesothosaurus,* but it had larger feet and various-sized teeth. It fed differently to *Lesothosaurus.* Instead of just swallowing food, *Heterodontosaurus* chewed everything in its cheek. The long fangs at the sides of the dinosaur's mouth may have used to dig up plant roots from the ground.

HOW DO I SAY THAT?

● **HETERODONTOSAURUS**
  HET-ER-OH-DON'T-OH-SAW-RUS
● **LESOTHOSAURUS**
  LESS-OH-TOE-SAW-RUS
● **SCUTELLOSAURUS**
  SCOOT-ELL-OH-SAW-RUS

Lesothosaurus
This dinosaur was one of the smallest plant-eaters. It used its small, powerful arms to gather up leaves and other plant food to stuff into its mouth. It had lots of sharp, evenly spaced teeth and slender jaws.

Heterodontosaurus

A plant-eating dinosaur whose name means "mixed-tooth reptile." Unlike most dinosaurs, *Heterodontosaurus* had three kinds of teeth: sharp cutting teeth at the front of the jaw, fangs just behind these, and grinding teeth in its cheek. It may have fed on tough ferns.

FACTFILE: LESOTHOSAURUS

Lived: 200 to 190 million years ago

Group: Ornithopoda

Size: 3 feet long

Weight: 22 pounds

Discovery: 1964, Lesotho, southern Africa

Diet: herbivore

Special features: small size, strong legs

Name means: "Lesotho reptile"

1. *Lesothosaurus*
2. *Heterodontosaurus* 3. *Scutellosaurus*

Scutellosaurus

With longer arms than *Lesothosaurus*, this dinosaur may have walked on all fours. It had an extremely long tail and regular, oval-shaped armor plates all over its body.

WHERE DID THEY LIVE?

Heterodontosaurus and *Lesothosaurus*

Scutellosaurus

SPEEDY & BIRDLIKE

It was once thought that hypsilophodontids lived in trees, grasping branches with their feet like giant birds.

The best-known hypsilophodontid is *Hypsilophodon*. When the first fossils of *Hypsilophodon* were found in 1849, scientists thought that they were the bones of a young *Iguanodon*. After more fossils were found, scientists realized this was a completely new dinosaur. Other hypsilophodontid fossils have been found all over the world. The biggest hypsilophodontid was *Tenontosaurus* from North America.

Hypsilophodontids were small and agile dinosaurs, with long, slender four-toed back legs. They had short front legs and stubby five-fingered hands. Their long fingers and toes led scientists to think that hypsilophodonitids might have been good at climbing trees. However, the muscles in their legs indicate that they were probably fast land runners. Hypsilophodontids had powerful jaws and grinding teeth. This helped them to chew tough plant material efficiently.

WHERE DID THEY LIVE?

● *Dryosaurus* and *Tenontosaurus*
● *Hypsilophodon*

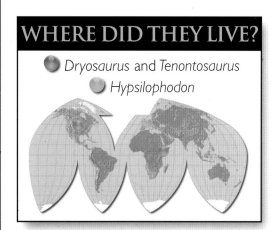

Hypsilophodon
This dinosaur had strong back legs and a horny beak for snipping off leaves. Hypsilodophodon had four fingers and a little spike on each foot.

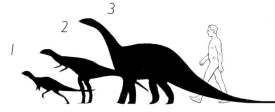

1. Dryosaurus 2. Hypsilophodon   3. Tenontosaurus

Tenontosaurus

A much bigger dinosaur than other hypsilophodontids, Tenontosaurus weighed around one ton. It had a powerful tail, which might have been used to strike attacking predators, such as Deinonychus.

FACTFILE: HYPSILOPHODON

- Lived: 140 to 120 million years ago
- Group: Ornithopoda
- Size: 6 1/2 feet long
- Weight: 110 pounds
- Discovery: 1849, England
- Diet: herbivore
- Special features: strong legs, beak
- Name means: "high-ridged tooth"

Dryosaurus

Like Hypsilophodon, Dryosaurus had a horny beak, but it had no front teeth. With its powerful back legs, this dinosaur was able to wander great distances, and the species spread all over the world.

HOW DO I SAY THAT?

DRYOSAURUS
DRY-OH-SAW-RUS

HYPSILOPHODON
HIP-SIL-OAF-OH-DON

TENONTOSAURUS
TEN-ONT-OH-SAW-RUS

ORNITHOPODS

Hypsilophodon was one of the most successful small ornithopods. Hypsilophodonitids were similar to iguanodontids such as *Iguanodon*. However, hypsilophodonitids had smaller, more sharply pointed teeth and a horny beak. They also had few teeth at the front of their jaws, and sometimes even no teeth at all. Many of today's plant-eating animals do not have teeth at the front of their mouths. Sheep, for example, snip off grass by pressing their tongue against a bony plates in the roof of their mouths.

DINO DICTIONARY

- **Femur:** the thigh bone
- **Carnivore:** a meat-eating animal

Hypsilophodon

THE ORNITHOPODS:

- *Dryosaurus*
- *Heterodontosaurus*
- *Hypsilophodon*
- *Lesothosaurus*
- *Scutellosaurus*
- *Tenontosaurus*

Running machine
Hypsilophodon *was a typical fast-running dinosaur. Its skeleton shows that with its backbone level, and its legs pumping away below,* Hypsilophodon *may have been able to run at top speed for long distances. The weight of its body in front and the tail behind were equal, so* Hypsilophodon *balanced like a seesaw over its back legs.*

INTERNET LINKS

http://www.dinosauria.com
A great virtual museum especially for kids, with links to even more sites.

http://www.dinosaur.org/frontpage.html
Read some informative articles and catch up on the latest news from the dinosaur world.

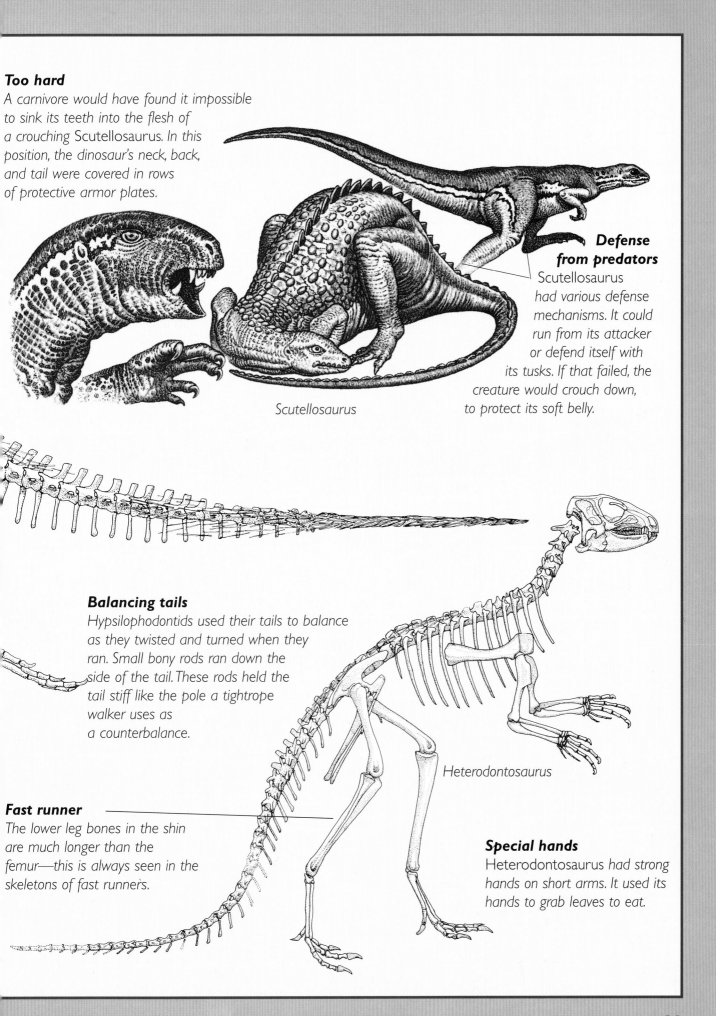

Too hard

A carnivore would have found it impossible to sink its teeth into the flesh of a crouching Scutellosaurus. In this position, the dinosaur's neck, back, and tail were covered in rows of protective armor plates.

Scutellosaurus

Defense from predators

Scutellosaurus had various defense mechanisms. It could run from its attacker or defend itself with its tusks. If that failed, the creature would crouch down, to protect its soft belly.

Balancing tails

Hypsilophodontids used their tails to balance as they twisted and turned when they ran. Small bony rods ran down the side of the tail. These rods held the tail stiff like the pole a tightrope walker uses as a counterbalance.

Heterodontosaurus

Fast runner

The lower leg bones in the shin are much longer than the femur—this is always seen in the skeletons of fast runners.

Special hands

Heterodontosaurus had strong hands on short arms. It used its hands to grab leaves to eat.

HORNLESS DINOSAURS

Early ceratopsians were small, two-legged dinosaurs that were unlike their giant relatives, but they lived in a similar way.

Most of the horn-faced dinosaurs, like *Triceratops* and *Styracosaurus*, were large, four-legged, tanklike animals with huge heads, neck frills, and sharp beaks. But the first ceratopsian, *Psittacosaurus*, was human-sized and stood upright on its back legs. Unlike the later ceratopsians, *Psittacosaurus* had no horns. Neither did it sport a big, bony neck frill. Its long legs and powerful grasping hands were similar to those found in ornithopods, such as *Hypsilophodon*. So what made it a ceratopsian? The clue is in the shape of its mouth—it was curved like a parrot's beak.

Skeleton

Psittacosaurus was a slender, two-legged dinosaur, like most ornithopods. However, the sturdy front legs may have been used for walking. The hooked beak suggests that Psittacosaurus ate tough plant food, maybe even tree branches.

WHERE DID THEY LIVE?

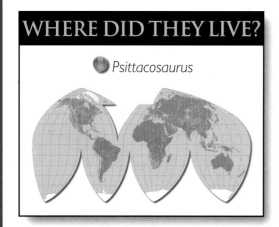

Psittacosaurus

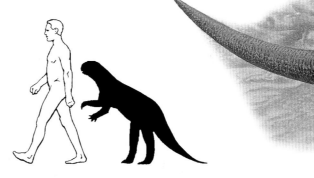

Psittacosaurus

FACTFILE: PSITTACOSAURUS

- Lived: 100 to 90 million years ago
- Group: Ceratopsia
- Size: 6 feet long
- Weight: 110 pounds
- Discovery: 1922, Mongolia
- Diet: herbivore
- Special features: parrot-like beak, strong hands
- Name means: "parrot reptile"

Plant-eater
Psittacosaurus *fed on leaves and fruit from trees, which it nipped off with its beak and then crushed and sliced at the back of its mouth.*

Little dinosaurs
Baby Psittacosaurus skeletons were tiny—about the same size as a pigeon. Young dinosaurs had much weaker jaws than adults, so they probably ate tender shoots and berries.

HOW DO I SAY THAT?

PSITTACOSAURUS
SIT-AK-OH-SAW-RUS

31

INDEX